CW00863956

How to Study the Bible

By

Joseph Kearney

This book is dedicated to all who know the TRUTH (Jesus Christ) and to all who want to know more about Him and His Church.

This book is printed in the United States of America

ISBN # 978-0-359-82259-1

Contents

Introduction

Houston, we have a problem! Most people, whether they are Protestant or Catholic or from some other religion, have never read the Bible. So if a person has no interest in reading the Bible, why would they want to study it?

This is why so many Churches, especially Catholic, do not conduct Bible Studies for its members. However, the ones that take the first step and try a study, find very quickly that people are actually thirsting for knowledge.

This book is intended to only enhance someone's experience. It is not meant to replace any particular way a Church or private Bible Study conducts their teaching.

There are numerous study guides, books,videos,Bible versions and commentaries on how to study the Bible. I recommend a combination of them all.

The Holy Spirit

In order for anyone to have a good and by "good"I mean a "spiritual" understanding and study of Sacred Scripture we must know the Author and accept the Author and all of His teachings, not just the ones we "feel" like accepting.

We are all on a "Journey" to heaven. We cannot "think" our way into heaven. Just by thinking we will be in heaven will never get us there!

Therefore, we must learn something about the Third Person of the Holy Trinity of whom Jesus stated will be our "Teacher."

As the Catechism of our Church states; "Sacred Scripture must be read and interpreted in light of the same Spirit by whom it was written."

This "same Spirit is the"same Spirit", that instituted the Church in 33 A.D. along with the Seven Sacraments.

The Catechism goes on to tell us many more "musts" for those of us who are In Christ and who have His Holy Spirit in our hearts.

We must never take a verse from Sacred Scripture out of context. By taking a verse out of context, we are allowing Satan to bring doubts and confusion into the Holy Word of God.

By listening to those who love to "tickle" ears for profit is one way of bringing doubt and confusion into the Sacred Writings.

We must also read and study Sacred Scripture in the light of the Sacred Tradition of the Church. What did the early Christians believe? What did the early Church Fathers believe? What was the understanding and teaching that has been handed down for over two thousand years?

We must also know the "truths" of our faith and find out if the Bible is in accordance with these "truths"?

We must learn the “senses” of Scripture.

Basically, there are two “senses” of Scripture. 1) Literal and 2) Spiritual.

For those of us living in present day America our usual language is English. We can understand many things by learning this language, we can read, write, and get many certificates and degrees. However, the Bible was not written in our language and we must not try to interpret it in our language.

The Bible was mostly written in the languages of its writers. The three languages that make up most of the Old and New Testament are Greek, Hebrew and Aramaic. Fortunately, for those of us alive today we have many Bible versions that have been translated for us from these languages. And of course, the internet is a great research tool for all languages, and what the meaning of them were in various cultures.

So, the Literal Sense (or meaning) must be learned from the languages they were written along with the culture of the time.

The Spiritual Sense has three components; 1) Allegorical 2) Moral 3 Anagogical

The Allegorical Sense allows us to see the Author and Finisher of our Faith all throughout Salvation History from Genesis to the Revelation of Jesus Christ. For example; the Greek word “allegorein” meaning to speak “figuratively”, as when God created the first man and woman, Adam and Eve, we can see His plan to right the wrong of their sin by giving us a New Adam in Jesus Christ and a New Eve in His Mother Mary.

The Moral Sense is probably the most used and confused.

To be a Moral person one must reach a level of maturity in Christ.

It does not mean to throw Scripture verses at people like one is using a whip.

All scripture is inspired by God and is useful for teaching, for refutation, for correction, and for training in righteousness, so that one, who belongs to God may be competent, equipped for every good work. 2 Timothy 3:16-17.

An example of a Moral sense are the Ten Commandments. These are in the Bible. One of the Commandments is "Thou Shall Not Kill", therefore we can clearly see that it is morally reprehensible to kill anyone especially if they are an innocent child in the womb of its mother.

The Anagogical Sense is interpreting Scripture within the framework of seeing what is above than what is here on earth. The Greek for this word means to "climb" or "ascend."

Therefore, this Sense teaches us about the afterlife and things to come, as in the Revelation of Jesus Christ chapter twenty-one.

The Holy Spirit will lead us into all truth in the Word of God. Before we begin to read, listen, or study the Bible we must pray to the Holy Spirit and ask Him to help us understand.

Asking the Holy Spirit for help to understand His Word is an act of our "will." An action that will begin to lead us into a serious following of Jesus. Prayer is a gift from God, and praying to God for help is an act of humility, an acknowledgement that understanding His word is more than just a mental exercise but rather reading Scripture daily helps us to grow in knowledge of Him.

The Bible is more than just a book or an adventure through Salvation History, it can be used for a personal need and or desire that each person can experience for themselves.

The Holy Spirit of God leads us into a personal relationship with His Son Our Lord Jesus Christ. And every person's relationship with Him is unique. The Holy Spirit may allow you to enter into a Gospel scene where you can identify with one of the characters, and someone else can be lead to see an answer to a problem.

Always keep your heart open to the Holy Spirit for He will never fail. God has never refused anyone who desires to be close to Him.

You must be made aware that even the most Saintly people have experienced what is known as the" Dark Night of the Soul", these are times when we don't want to pray, don't want to read or study, and may even feel as if the Lord has left us. But it is during these times that the Holy Spirit is working in our inner selves more than ever. So don't become discouraged when you come to this point in your Spiritual Walk because it will pass, and you may become more teachable, more aware of your lack of holiness, and or you may just desire to live in peace and joy that the Lord has bestowed on you and refrain from doing anything else.

Your movement from darkness to light may give you the inner love of God to such an extent that you can see this love all around you and in everything God created. Maybe your journey has brought you to the point of just wanting to live in love and share the love in whatever way God has chosen for you.

Listen to these words of Jesus; " I am the way, the truth and the life. No one comes to the Father except through me". John 14:6

"And I will ask the Father, and He will give you an advocate to help you and be with you forever the Spirit of Truth". John 14:16-17.

"But the Advocate, the Holy Spirit, whom the Father will send in my name, will teach you all things and will remind you of everything I have said to you. Peace I leave with you; my peace I give you. I do not give to you as the world gives. Do not let your hearts be troubled and do not be afraid". John 14:26-27.

Knowledge

We must always check our motivation when we approach an individual or group Bible study. What do we expect the outcome to be for us at the end of the study? What questions do we have about the Bible? What do we expect to learn? Will we have an open mind?

The Bible tells us that many perish for lack of knowledge, so it is imperative that we gain knowledge of the Bible because it is the only place on this earth that tells us the truth about our creator, our creation, our laws, our right way to live and how to live "forever"to have "Eternal Life."

We must never try to interpret the Bible without guidance from the Church. Jesus did not come down to earth to write a book. He came to start a Church. He gave His Authority to interpret His Word during the Church Age, which is from

His first coming to His second coming. His Church can be traced back to 33 A.D. His Church has had the teachings from this time until now of all its Apostles, Bishops, Deacons, Priests and Popes.

Most of these teachings can be found on the internet, in bookstores, in the Catechism and on the website for the United States Conference of Catholic Bishops.

You can also find great studies on the Bible by great Bible Scholars like Scott Hahn, Jeff Cavins and the University of Navarre.

You can go to many good Bible websites that have in depth teaching such as Agapebiblestudy.org, Verbum.com and Catholic.com

Look up any words you do not understand in a secular dictionary and in a Bible Dictionary.

Here are the versions of the Bible I use: 1) The New American Bible 2) The New Jerusalem Bible 3) The Revised Standard Version 4) The New International Version 5) The New King James Version 6) The Chronological Study Bible

There are numerous Bible versions and you need to choose those that do not allow for individual interpretation but allow the Holy Spirit to lead you to the Truth and His Church. Stay away from any "paraphrased" versions.

Always check your motivation for studying the Bible. Ask yourself some questions like, do you want to learn about Jewish roots in Christianity? Do you want to learn about the first man and woman? Do you want to learn the history of God's chosen people? Do you want to know more about God the Father? Do you want to know more about the Son of God? Do you want to know more about the Holy Spirit?

Do you want to know more about the early Church? Do you want to know how to pray? Do you want to know Angels? Do you want to know the Blessed Virgin Mary? Do you want to know what happened? Do you want to know what is happening? Do you want to know what is going to happen? Do you want to know how to live a holy life?

As you can see, there are many questions you can ask yourself that make good reason for you to study Sacred Scripture.

Here are some ways to read the Bible.

The first five books of the Bible gave the Israelites stability and assurance in their walk with the Lord. And then you can learn about their history before their exile by reading Joshua to 2 Kings and subsequently you can read about their history during the postexilic period by reading I Chronicles to Maccabees.

Read religious historical novels Tobit, Judith, Esther.

Learn about wisdom from the wisdom books, Job, Psalms, Proverbs, Ecclesiastes, Song of Solomon, Wisdom of Solomon, and Sirach.

Read the prophetic books, Isaiah, Jeremiah, Lamentations, Baruch, Ezekiel, Daniel, Hosea, Joel, Amos, Obadiah, Jonah, Micah, Nahum, Habakkuk, Zephaniah, Haggai, Zechariah, and Malachi.

Read about the Ministry of Jesus, His teachings and miracles, His death and Resurrection in the Four Gospels, Matthew, Mark, Luke and John.

Read about what the Apostles of Jesus did after He ascended to heaven in the Book of Acts.

Read about how evangelisation spread to many parts of the world by the Apostles and the Apostle Paul in the Book of Romans, I and II Corinthians, the Letter to the Galatians, to the Ephesians, to the Phillipians, to the Colossians and I and II Thessalonians.

Read the Pastoral Letters from the Apostle Paul to the Church Leaders in I and II Timothy, the Letter to Titus, the Letter to Philemon, and the Letter to the Hebrews.

Read a book by the Apostle James and a book by the first Pope the I and II Letters of Peter, the I, II, and III Letters of the Apostle John, and the Letter of Jude.

And read about how things will end in the Book of Revelation of Jesus Christ.

The Word of God is Eternal; you can never learn and or study everything there is to know about it.

One of the beauties about the Church is that it has an abundance of writings and teachings on the Word of God to such an extent that it also appears to be eternal in nature. The wealth of knowledge one can learn about the Bible, and all things of God is so vast in the Church that you would spend your life reading and studying and still never reach the end.

Meditation

Meditation not as the world gives, but as one of the teachings in the Church, Lectio Divina.

Before I explain this teaching, you must first learn the discipline by picking up a Bible version and reading it in a relaxed manner.

To do this reading in a relaxed manner you need to turn off all noise.

Once you have developed a daily relaxed reading of the Word, then you can begin to ask questions, to write down notes and seek knowledge.

You can “go deeper”, by meditating on the Word of God. And to help you the Church gives you Lectio Divina an ancient Christian way to pray. Once you develop this way of prayerfully reading Holy Scripture, you will eventually realize the true nature of God and His creation = Love. You will develop deep in your being the reason for your life and for every other creation, to know, to love, and serve God.

This will bring you into a place you never dreamed possible, of being able to read the Word of God in union with the Holy Spirit of God. Your reading will forever remain "Spiritual" in nature. You will no longer seek to read in quantity, or to read at a certain pace, but to devour into your heart every Word of Sacred Scripture.

You will be able to grow into a personal relationship with Jesus Christ because He loves you.

Always remember to "be still", "be in silence", "take deep breaths", rest in Him and allow Jesus to wrap His loving arms around you.

Learn to pray like Jesus, He would often go into the hills to pray, He would spend the night in prayer, and He would rise before dawn to pray.

Seek and you will find, knock and the door will be opened for you. Jesus is waiting.

Lectio Divina has several components, 1) Read a verse or verses very slowly and carefully 2) Pray (especially in the Spirit) over them and have a conversation with God 3) Meditate by listening to what God is saying and look for the spiritual reality being conveyed.

4) Contemplate what you have just done while resting in the presence of God. 5) Take some action like telling someone what you have learned or write down notes to share.

St John of the Cross has a great insight taken from the Gospel of Luke 11:9, seek in Reading, find in Meditation, knock in Prayer and it will be opened to you in Contemplation.

Lectio Divina is a process, not an instruction to be done in a regimented way. But an engagement with God that produces deep prayer over a period of time. If you have an open heart that only wants to know, love, and serve God more than anything else in the world, He will allow these to happen for you.

Let us go over the steps we take to become closer to God, 1) Reading and Listening to the Word of God (like listening to the readings of His Word during Mass). 2) Reflecting on His Word - Meditation. 3) Allow the Word to touch our hearts - Contemplation. Here we see how our free will is used to Read and Listen so that our Reflection (meditation) can be used by our imagination and intellect to bring us into the Spiritual Realm of Contemplation where we can live the words of St John the Baptist, “He must increase, I must decrease.”

Sources

The Catechism of the Catholic Church

A Catholic Guide to the Bible
By Oscar Lukefahr C.M.

Too Deep for Words
By Thelma Hall, r.c.

The New American Bible

The Revised Standard Version

The New International Version

Disclaimer

This book is not endorsed or affiliated with any Church, Denomination, or any other Christian organization.

As a Catholic and a member of the Church, I tried my best to not allow any heresy to be a part of the book.

I am a layperson who is allowed to share the Word of God in the spirit of Vatican II and in accordance with Canon Law #208 and # 215.

My other books can be found at lulu.com/rtcm49

CPSIA information can be obtained
at www.ICGtesting.com
Printed in the USA
BVHW031001100919
557937BV00007B/4/P